# THE KHABAROVSK WAR CRIMES TRIAL

*Unearthing Biological Warfare in WWII*

Pacific Atrocities Education

# THE KHABAROVSK WAR CRIMES TRIAL

*Unearthing Biological Warfare in WWII*

**JENNY CHAN**

# THE KHABAROVSK WAR CRIMES TRIAL:
## Unearthing Biological Warfare in WWII

Editor:
**Catherine R. Sloan**

Cover Illustration:
**Maja Kopunovic**

Paperback ISBN: 978-1-947766-19-8

E-book ISBN: 978-1-947766-15-0

# Table of Contents

**Chapter One**

# Background Information on Unit 731

Of 3607 members of Unit 731, twelve were brought to trial at Khabarovsk. Did justice ever prevail?

Unit 731 was a biological and chemical warfare research unit of the Imperial Japanese Army during WWII. It was in this unit that the Japanese were getting ready for germ warfare. It established headquarters in Harbin, Manchuria.

Although Harbin belonged to China, it always had close ties to Russia due to the close proximity of its location. Russia had enjoyed working in Manchuria as it provides ports with no ice and milder temperatures compared to their mother country. From 1896-1903, Harbin grew from a small village into a metropolitan city due to the construction of the Chinese Eastern Railway financed by the Russian Empire and backed by French bankers. It was later extended to connect to the Trans-Siberian Railway.[1] At the time, many Chinese immigrated to Manchuria

---

[1] "History & Facts of Harbin." *History of Harbin, Timeline & Chronology Events & Facts in Harbin, China Ice Festival*, www.harbinice.com/fact-v7-history-facts-of-harbin.html.

because it promised a better way of life than that possible in their ancestral village or promised by the decaying Ching dynasty. The Russia Empire was able to provide the Chinese who fled their homes work for the new railroad, new factories, and the new land.

Meanwhile, in Japan, industrialization was happening as a result of Commodore Matthew Perry's visit. The US military had forced Japan to open its ports to connect to the western world. It also began to act on its ambition to conquer the world to acquire more resources. Through industrialization, Japan eventually was able to challenge military power from the West.

Japan and Russia were engaged in the Russo-Japanese War during 1904-5, for which Russia used Harbin as a military base in Northeastern China. They fought in the Yellow Sea, the Sea of Japan, the Korean Peninsula, and Manchuria. The Empire of Japan won the war, which led to the Treaty of Portsmouth, negotiated by U.S. President Theodore Roosevelt. The Portsmouth Treaty gave the Empire of Japan control of Korea as well as a part of Manchuria, including Port Arthur and the railway that connected it with the rest of the region and the southern half of Sakhalin Island.[2] Russia's loss of the war also meant that the days of the Czar were limited.

By December 1918, over 100,000 Russian White Guards who were defeated during the Russian Civil War retreated to Harbin. Harbin then became a major center of White Russian emigres and had the largest population

---

[2] *U.S. Department of State*, history.state.gov/milestones/1899-1913/portsmouth-treaty.

of Russians outside of Soviet Union by the time the USSR (Union of Soviet Socialist Revolution) was formed in 1922.[3]

As Japan invaded Manchuria in 1931, the Empire of Japan established Manchukuo and took control of Harbin. In order to stage a puppet government, they put in Prince Puyi, who had been overthrown at the age of 6 by Sun Yat-sen in the 1911 revolution for the founding of modern China. He was installed by the Japanese as a puppet emperor in 1932.

Many Japanese saw great opportunities in Manchuria as it became a Japanese colony, and it offered more opportunities for power-hungry scientists. The conquest of Manchuria allowed the Japanese Empire to grow its confidence and let ultra-nationalistic officials take over the government. As an opportunist, Ishii seized this opportunity and used his family's influence to obtain funding from the War Ministry to establish a biological weapons lab.

His subordinate, Kajitsuka Ryuji, described his rise to fame in an interrogation on October 24, 1949, as follows: "Ishii Shiro, born around 1893 in the Prefecture of Chiba, comes from the family of a wealthy landowner, and in 1919-20 graduated from the College of Medicine of the Imperial University in the town of Kyoto. He then entered the service of the Japanese Army as a volunteer. Soon after, he applied for enlistment in regular army service. Half a year later, he received his first commission as a lieutenant and was appointed army physician in

---

[3] *World War I: The Definitive Encyclopedia and Document Collection.* p. 570 Abc-Clio, 2015.

an army unit. From there, he was transferred to the First Military Hospital in the city of Tokyo, where I became acquainted with him in October 1922 as a colleague. From April 1924 to March 1926 he was a postgraduate student in pathology and bacteriology at the university from which he had graduated in 1919-20. Then, until April 1928, he worked as a resident physician at the military hospital in the town of Kyoto, from which he was sent abroad on a mission, returning at the end of 1930. On his mission abroad, he visited almost all the countries of Europe, including the U.S.S.R., where he acquainted himself with the work of medical research institutes in Moscow and Leningrad. Upon his return from abroad, Ishii became an instructor of epidemiology at the Military Medical Academy of the Japanese Army in the city of Tokyo. From this post, he was appointed Chief of Detachment 731 in 1936 by an order of the Japanese Minister for War. His rank at the time was Lieutenant Colonel of the Medical Service. In 1931, after returning from his mission abroad, in the circle of his comrades at the Military Medical Academy, of whom I was one, as well as among authoritative and influential officers of the Japanese General Staff, Ishii began to propagate Japan's need to prepare for bacteriological warfare... Beginning with 1933, Major General Nagata, Chief of the Military Affairs Division of the Japanese Ministry for War, supported Ishii's idea and beginning with 1935, also Colonel Suzuki Yorimichi, Chief of the 1st Section of the Strategical Division of the Japanese General Staff. All these circumstances, as well as the fact that Ishii was a big specialist, led to his being appointed Chief of Detachment 731, and upon taking up this post he began research on weapons of bacteriological warfare."

Ishii's reasoning involved a desire to expand the Japanese Empire in a more efficient manner. He was able to establish the headquarters for his biological weapons lab, otherwise known as Unit 731. Its official name was "The Water Supply and Prophylaxis Administration of the Kwantung Army."

The success of his unit allowed Ishii to rise through the ranks quickly, and become a general by the end of the war. The unit routinely performed human experimentation, developed chemical and biological weapons, and produced bacteriological weapons in times of warfare. Due to Ishii's fascination with Japan's victory in the Russo-Japanese War, he gave his lab the nickname "Togo Unit," after one of the greatest naval heroes of Japan, Togo Heihachiro. He sometimes also signed his name as Captain Togo Hajime.[4]

The Khabarovsk War Crime Trial consisted of hearings held between the 25th and 31st of December, 1949. The depositions alone filled 18 volumes with 400 pages of interrogations and documents gathered in the investigations four years after the war was over. Although there were 1000-1600 audience members each day for the trial,

---

[4] "Factories of Death: Japanese Biological Warfare 1932-45 and the American Cover-Up." *Factories of Death: Japanese Biological Warfare 1932-45 and the American Cover-Up*, by Sheldon H. Harris, Routledge, 2015, p. 23.

it was not covered by Western media because Khabarovsk was a remote destination for any foreigners to visit.

The scientists who worked at Unit 731 were top scientists of the time recruited in Japan. The twelve former personnel of the biological weapons lab who were tried during the Khabarovsk Trial were: Yamada Otozoo, Kajitsuka Ryuji, Takahashi Takaatsu, Katashima Kiyoshi, Nishi Toshihide, Karasawa Tomio, Onoue Masao, Sato Shunji, Hirazakura Zensaku, Mitomo Kazuo, Kikuchi Norimitsu, and Kurushima Yuji. The defendants were charged with allegedly manufacturing and employing bacteriological weapons.

However, the Cold War that set in right after WWII led to politics that made it hard for justice to prevail. As the United States and the Soviet Union entered into the Cold War era, the fate of the captured Japanese soldiers became more of a political poker game.

Although there were 3607 members of Unit 731, only twelve were brought to trial at Khabarovsk, otherwise known as the Khabarovsk War Crime Trial. Some were able to play their cards strategically and became witnesses instead of defendants in court. Ultimately, the leader of the operation, General Ishii, escaped this trial by faking his own death, and was later found by the CIA. He was able to trade his research results for immunity with the United States and lived a peaceful life until dying of throat cancer in 1959.

## Chapter Two

# Information on the Defendants

**Yamada Otozoo** was born in 1881 in Tokyo. He became a Commander-in-Chief in 1944, a post he held until the end of the war, serving the Japanese Kwantung Army and ranked as a General. He supervised the activity of Unit 731 and 100 in order to prepare for bacteriological warfare. His responsibilities included inspecting the units, monitoring the situations in the units through reports from his staff, and taking measures to keep the units in a constant state of military readiness.

He stated in his testimony, "Detachment 731 was directly subordinated to me, as Commander-in-Chief of the Kwantung Army. I had charge of the tactical direction of Detachment 731 in all matters concerning the production of bacteriological weapons and their use. This meant that if the necessity arose to employ bacteriological weapons against enemy forces, it was I that would have to give the order to this effect, since Detachment 731 was a special combat unit under my control."

**Kajitsuka Ryuji** was born in 1888 in the town of Tajiri. He was trained as a physician and bacteriologist, and was the Chief of Medical Administration for the Japanese Kwantung Army starting in 1939 and ranked as a Lieutenant General of the Medical Service by the end of the war.

He was an early believer in biological weapons. Even as early as 1931, Kajitsuka was an active supporter of Ishii Shiro. He became one of the initiators of research on methods of employing bacteriological weapons. By 1934-1936, he became the head of a division of the Medical Administration of the Japanese War Ministry. He then recruited the necessary expert staff for Unit 731. He was well informed on the activities of Unit 731.

His testimony states the following, "... I was well informed ... that Detachment 731 experimented continuously on human beings with the object of discovering the most effective types of bacteriological weapons. I knew that Detachment 731 employed bacteriological weapons in 1941-42 against the Chinese Army and Chinese civilians."

**Takahashi Takaatsu** was born in 1888 in the town of Honze. He was trained as a biological chemist. He was Chief of the Veterinary Service of the Japanese Kwantung Army from 1944 and by the end of the war, he was ranked as Lieutenant General of the Veterinary Service. His responsibilities included directly supervising the activities of Unit 100, and he had an active role in preparing for bacteriological warfare. His testimony stated the following: "I directed the preparations for bacteriological warfare and bacteriological sabotage against the Soviet Union... I gave orders for Detachment 100 to prepare, and controlled its production of the bacteria of glanders and anthrax and the virus of cattle plague and mosaic disease, with a view to their employment in bacteriological warfare and bacteriological sabotage against the Soviet Union."

**Kawashima Kiyoshi** was born in 1893 in the village of Hasunuma. He was trained as a physician and bacteriologist. By the end of the war, he was the Chief of the Production Division of Detachment 731 of the Japanese Kwantung ranking as Army Major General of the Medical Service from 1941 to 1943. He was responsible for organizing the mass production of bacteriological weapons and human experimentation.

His testimony states the following, "In April 1941, just after I arrived to take up my post in the detachment, I inspected the prison, and in one of the cells I saw two Russian women, one of whom had a year-old child, born in the detachment's prison. During the period I was with the detachment these women were alive. Their subsequent fate I do not know, but at any rate, these women could not have left the prison alive, and the same lot as that of the other prisoners must have befallen them... I acknowledge that the methods we employed of experimenting on human beings and of their mass annihilation by the action of lethal bacteria were barbarous and a crime against humanity."

**Nishi Toshihide** was born in 1904 in the village of Hiwaki. He was trained as a physician and bacteriologist. He was the Chief of the Training and Education Division

(Branch 673) of Detachment 731 of the Japanese Kwantung Army starting in January 1943 and ranked as Lieutenant Colonel of the Medical Service by the time the war ended. He supervised the training of personnel for special units intended for bacteriological warfare. During the preliminary investigation, Nishi stated, "I am aware that the war that was being prepared for would have caused great sacrifice of life among the civilian population, that these weapons of bacteriological warfare and the testing of bacteriological weapons on living people by forcible infection were criminal and inhuman."

**Karasawa Tomio** was born in 1911 in the village of Toyosato, and was trained as a physician and bacteriologist. He became the sectional chief of the Production Division of Detachment 731 of the Japanese Kwantung Army in 1939, ranking as Major of Medical Service by the end of the war. His responsibilities included mass-producing bacteriological weapons, supplying bacteria to the special expeditions in Central China from Unit 731, and testing lethal bacteria on prisoners. During an interrogation, he stated, "From 1939 to 1944 I did indeed serve in Detachment 731 of the Japanese Kwantung Army in Manchuria, which detachment carried on active research in devising the most perfect methods of producing bacteria on a mass scale and of using them as means of bacteriological warfare. In performing its function of preparing to conduct bacteriological warfare, the detachment systematically performed experiments in forcibly infecting with contagious diseases people whom the Japanese

Gendarmerie sent to Detachment 731 to be done away with."

**Onoue Masao** was born in 1910 in the town of Kome-notsu. He was trained as a physician and bacteriologist. By the end of the war, he was the Chief of Branch 643 of Detachment 731 of the Japanese Kwantung Army, having assumed that position in October 1943 and was ranked as Major of Medical Service at the end of the war.

He directly supervised research work on bacteriological weapons for the most effective military use as well as producing them on a mass scale. His testimony states the following, "Branch 643, which was under my charge, bred rodents and plague-carrying fleas, which were consigned to Detachment 731, where they were used for the manufacture of bacteriological weapons."

**Sato Shunji** was born in 1896 in the town of Toyohashi, into a family of nobles. He was a physician and bacteriologist. He graduated in 1931 with the degree Doctor of Medical Sciences with a thesis on "Experimental Infusion of Glucose Solutions." From 1941-1943, he was the Chief of Nami and Ei detachments. From 1944 until the end of the war, he was the Chief of the Medical Service of the 5th Army of the Japanese Kwantung Army, ranking as Major General of the Medical Service, where he supervised Branch 643 of Unit 731.

His responsibilities as the Chief of Nami and Ei detachments included researching and producing bacteriological weapons. Then, as Chief of the Medical Service of the 5th Army, he actively assisted and supported Branch

643 in increasing output of bacteriological material, and issued a special order to the troops of the 5th Army to procure rodents for the branch.

In his testimony, he stated, "As Chief of Detachment Ei 1644, I directed the detachment's work in devising bacteriological weapons and producing them on a mass scale. For this purpose, the Nanking Detachment Ei 1644 was supplied with high-capacity equipment and with bacteriological experts and it produced lethal bacteria on a mass scale. It is true that under my direction, the Training Division of the Nanking Detachment Ei 1644 every year trained about 300 bacteriologists with the object of employing them in bacteriological warfare. From March 1944 onwards, as Chief of the Medical Service of the 5th Army of the Japanese Kwantung Army, I rendered Branch 643 of Detachment 731 active assistance and support in increasing the output of bacteriological material."

**Hirazakura Zensaku** was born 1916 in the village of Kanazawa. He was a veterinary surgeon. From July 1942, he was a member of Detachment 100 of the Japanese Kwantung Army, ranking as Lieutenant of the Veterinary Service by the end of the war. His responsibilities included researching, mass producing bacteriological weapons for use in an attack on the USSR, and surveying and directing a sabotage group made up of personnel from Unit 100. During an interrogation, he stated, "Being a veterinary surgeon, as a researcher, first in the 1st Section of the 2nd Division of the detachment, and later in the 6$^{th}$ Section of the same division formed in December 1943, I studied the action of glanders and anthrax germs, engaged in the breeding of these germs, and took part in devising all sorts of methods of using these germs in bacteriological warfare."

**Mitomo Kazuo** was born in 1924 in the village of Haraya. He was a member of Detachment 100 of the Japanese Kwantung Army from April 1941 and ranked as Senior Sergeant by 1944. His duties included breeding of lethal bacteria for use in bacteriological warfare, sabotage against the USSR, and putting prisoners to painful death by testing the reaction of various bacteriological weapons upon them. He stated during an interrogation on December 6$^{th}$, 1949, "I voluntarily joined Detachment 100 of the Kwantung Army which engaged in manufacturing germs of anthrax, glanders, cattle plague and sheep plague, and also that, knowing that these germs were being manufactured especially for the purpose of waging war against the Soviet Union, I took an active part in their manufacture in the special laboratory of Detachment 100. On joining the afore-mentioned detachment I went through a special course of training in the cultivation of the germs of anthrax and glanders, which I myself cultivated in an incubator that was especially assigned to me. I conducted this work throughout the whole period I was in the detachment, i.e., from April 1941 to October 1944."

**Kikuchi Norimitsu** was born in 1922 in the Prefecture of Ehime. After nine years of schooling, he worked as a laboratory assistant from April 1943 to August 1945 in Branch 643 of Detachment 731 of the Japanese Kwantung Army ranking as a corporal. His responsibilities included helping in research work on bacteriological weapons by cultivating typhoid and dysentery germs. He stated during an interrogation on December 6th, 1949, "I plead guilty to having, while serving in Branch 643 of Detachment 731 in the period from April 1943 to the day I was taken prisoner, engaged in the cultivation of the germs of typhoid, paratyphoid, dysentery and tuberculosis for the purpose of research on these germs and of studying their properties and ability to cause epidemics. While engaged in the cultivation of bacteria I studied the media on which they bred in order to procure a medium on which they could be cultivated faster and preserve their vitality for a longer period."

**Kurushima Yuji** was born in 1923 in the Prefecture of Kagawa in the village of Noo. After eight years of schooling, he started in October 1944 working as a laboratory orderly of Branch 162 of Detachment 731 of the Japanese Kwantung Army until the end of the war. His job was to cultivate cholera, typhoid, and other germs.

He stated during an interrogation conducted on December 10th, 1946, "It is true that after I was enrolled in the Japanese Army, and after going through general military training in the 97th Infantry Regiment, I, in April 1944, was sent to serve in Branch 162 of Detachment 731, located in Linkow. Soon after my arrival at this branch I realized from the nature of the work that was conducted and from the warnings I received about the secret character of the activities of Detachment 731 that, although Detachment 731 was officially supposed to be engaged with questions concerning water supply and prophylaxis, it actually engaged in breeding the germs of severe infectious diseases (typhoid, para-typhoid, cholera, plague, etc.), and also in breeding fleas and rodents for this purpose."

## Chapter Three

# Timeline of Japan's Aggression onto the Soviet Union

The Japanese Empire attacked the Soviet Union during the Pacific Asia War. According to the Japanese militarists' strategic plans for aggression, "the USSR was usually referred to as 'Target No. 1.'" By 1941, the Japanese Empire had an aggressive plan to attack the Soviet Union—called the Kantokuen Plan.

Here is the timeline of the Japanese Empire's aggression toward the USSR according to the Khabarovsk Trial. In 1931, Japanese armed forces provoked the so-called "Mukden incident" and thereafter invaded and occupied Manchuria. Manchuria became a springboard for attacks on the Soviet Union and China, and became the headquarters for a biological weapon laboratory headed by General Ishii Shiro.

In 1936, the Japanese military preparation for war intensified, and a biological weapon was deemed to be cost-effective for a total war. With a decree issued by Emperor Hirohito and funding by the War Ministry of Japan, two large bacteriological institutions were formed not only for evolving methods of waging biological warfare, but also for producing a weapon at a massive scale. Those institutions were Unit 731 and Unit 100, disguised with the following code names: "Water Supply and Prophylaxis Administration of the Kwantung Army" and "HippoEpizootic Administration of the Kwantung Army."

In 1937, Japanese troops, after provoking the so-called "Marco Polo Bridge incident" invaded China; in 1938, the Japanese military attacked the U.S.S.R. in the Lake Hasan area but was routed by the Soviet Army; In 1939, the Japanese imperialists attacked the Mongolian People's Republic, the friend of the U.S.S.R., in the Khal-khin-Gol area, but were likewise routed by the armed forces of the M.P.R. and the Soviet Union; At the end of 1941, the Japanese militarists brought Japan into the Second World War on the side of Hitler's Germany.

And after the war, the Nuremberg Trial (International Military Tribunal) and the Tokyo War Crimes Trial (International Military Tribunal of the Far East) attempted to bring war criminals to justice. However, unlike the International Military Tribunal, the International Military Tribunal of the Far East wasn't created by an international agreement.[1] It was made clear during the tribunal's proceedings that the Imperial Japanese Army was exerting aggression toward the Soviet Union.

In the preliminary research for the Khabarovsk Trial, it was established that during the aggression and preparations for aggression toward the Soviet Union and other

---

[1] "The Nuremberg Trial and the Tokyo War Crimes Trials (1945–1948)." *U.S. Department of State*, history.state.gov/milestones/ 1945-1952/nuremberg.

countries, the Japanese Empire had "employ[ed] a criminal means of mass extermination of human beings—the weapon of bacteriological warfare."

Further, during the preliminary investigation, it was clear that the Japanese General Staff and Ministry for War set up a bacteriological laboratory with Ishii Shiro as its leader after the seizure of Manchuria. The act of setting up a bacteriological weapon lab was ordered by Emperor Hirohito.

Kawashima Kiyoshi, a defendant in the trial, who was formerly Major General in the Japanese Army Medical Service, confirmed that Emperor Hirohito was the one providing the secret instructions. Furthermore, he confirmed that the Japanese General Staff and Ministry for War formed the two top-secret units for preparing and conducting bacteriological warfare in Manchuria as early as 1935-1936 with the zaibatsu supporting them.

This account was confirmed by an interrogation of Kajitsuka Ryuji on October 23, 1949: "Detachment 731 was formed by command of the Emperor of Japan Hirohito, issued in 1936... The Emperor's command was printed and copies of it were sent to all the units of the Japanese Army for the information of all the officers. I myself was shown this command and the detachment's personnel list accompanying it, and certified the fact with my private seal."

During an interrogation on October 24, 1949, Kajitsuka Ryuji continued telling what he knew about the structure of Unit 731. "Detachment 731 was reorganized in 1939-40 under a special secret decree issued by

Emperor Hirohito of Japan in 1939. I was acquainted with this decree at the Kwantung Army Headquarters approximately in February 1940, signing a pledge of secrecy. Besides this, by one or perhaps two secret decrees, issued by Emperor Hirohito in 1940, four branches of Detachment 731 were set up additionally in the second half of that year, to be located in the towns of Hailar and Sunyu, and at Hailin and Linkow stations, the dates of their formation being indicated. The appended tables of organization, signed by War Minister Tojo, showed that each of these branches had a personnel of up to 300 men. Orders issued by Japanese War Minister Tojo in accordance with the emperor's decrees listed the hospitals and Detachment 731 which assigned a definite number of army medical specialists, non-commissioned officers and privates. The orders also indicated that civilians might be employed, but no more than 30 percent of the entire personnel." His statement made it very clear that Unit 731 belonged to the Japanese military.

## Chapter Four

# The Difference Between Unit 731 and Unit 100

The two top-secret units were Unit 731 and Unit 100. They had many similarities, i.e., human experimentation, and they both had branches throughout the world. Here is a table to make the identification of the two units easier:

# UNIT 100

### VERSUS

# UNIT 731

## COMPARING THE 2 TOP-SECRET UNITS TO PREPARE AND CONDUCT BACTERIOLOGICAL WARFARE

## LEARN MORE AT PACIFICATROCITIES.ORG

| | |
|---|---|
| Unit 100 was headed by Major General Wakamatsu of the Veterinary Service. | Unit 731 was headed by Lietenant General Ishii Shiro in the Army Medical Service. |
| Its purpose was to conduct research about diseases originating from animals as well as spreading diseases via animal carrier. | Its purpose was to produce, test, deploy, and store biological weapon. |
| Its headquarter was located in Mokotan, Manchukuo. | Its headquarter was located in Harbin, Manchukuo. |
| It carried out sabotage measures such as infecting pastures, cattle and water sources with epidemic germs. | It carried out sabotage measures with plague-infected fleas via airplane, spread typhoid and paratyphoid germs into wells, marshes, and houses, and aerosprayed bubonic plague. |

The West often dismissed the Khabarovsk War Crimes Trial as "Communist Propaganda."[1] However, it was the first time scientists from the "Epidemic Prevention and Water Purification Department" of the Imperial Japanese Army (IJA) came forward with the crimes they committed during World War II. To confuse others about what their mission was, they frequently used the name, "Water Supply and Prophylaxis Administration of the Kwantung Army," or "Hippo-Epizootic Administration of the Kwantung Army." Although the mission was established in 1935-1936, it was not until 1941, after the Nazi Germany attack on the U.S.S.R. and the world was engaged in a full-blown war, that the institutions were renamed Unit 100 and Unit 731, and given more specific tasks and employed thousands of scientists, as stated previously.

The trial made clear to the public how these biological and chemical weapon divisions worked for the IJA at the time. Unit 100 and Unit 731 were both staffed by leading bacteriologists of Japan. They had numerous branches located in strategic areas. The Japanese Army Command funded both units for their research and development, which made the units direct subordinates of the Commander-in-Chief of the IJA.

It was proven by evidence in the trial that both Unit 731 and 100, as well as their branches, were subordinated to the Commander-in-Chief of the Kwantung Army, as is corroborated by an order issued on December 2,

---

[1] Nie, JB. J. Bioethical Inquiry (2004) 1: 32.
https://doi.org/10.1007/BF02448905

1940, by General Umezu Yoshijiro, on the formation of four new branches of Unit 731, which order is appended to the case.

Both of the units and their branches carried on systematic bacteriological research with the object of ascertaining: the types of germs that would be the most effective for use as bacteriological weapons, as well as the best method for breeding them on a mass scale, and techniques for utilizing them to exterminate large populations and cause economic damage by infecting cattle and crops too.

Unit 731 was quartered in a specially-built and strictly-guarded military containment in the vicinity of Ping-fan Station, 20 kilometers from the city of Harbin. It was a high-capacity institute for the preparation of bacteriological warfare, with about 3,000 scientific and technical personnel.

## The Eight Divisions of Unit 731

The 1st Division bred germs of plague, cholera, gas gangrene, anthrax, typhoid, paratyphoid fever, and other diseases in bacteriological warfare. The 2nd Division was more of an experimental division that conducted tests of unique weapons to disseminate germs. They worked on sprayers in the form of fountain pens and walking stickers, porcelain aerial bombs, and other weapons for the sabotage groups. They also controlled an aircraft unit with specially equipped planes and a proving ground near Anta Station (where they tested the effects of certain biological bombs). The 2$^{nd}$ Division also engaged in the cultivation and breeding of parasites designed to cause plague epidemics.

Although Unit 731 claimed that they were working at the "Epidemic Prevention and Water Purification Department" of the IJA, it is known that out of the eight divisions of Unit 731, only one of them (the 3$^{rd}$ Division) occupied themselves with the research of water supply and prophylaxis. But even so, that Division manufactured cases for bacteria shells known as "Ishii aerial bombs," which were used to drop plague-infected fleas from aircraft.

The 4$^{th}$ Division was a "factory" for mass production of germs and various bacteria. This division had high-capacity equipment, divided into two sections, each of which could produce germs independently. The main equipment of the first section consisted of four boilers, each of one-ton capacity, for the preparation of the culture medium for the bacteria, and 14 autoclaves for sterilizing the medium, each 3 meters long and 1.5 meters in diameter. Each autoclave could hold 30 cultivators of a special design invented by Ishii, the Chief of Detachment 731. This first section had two cooling chambers for the medium, each of which could hold 100 cultivators simultaneously. This section also had five thermostats with a total capacity of 620 Ishii cultivators.

The second section had two boilers with two-ton capacity each, eight autoclaves, each capable of containing 60 cultivators, and other equipment.

The division also had a special refrigerator for preserving the finished "product." Experts have calculated, on the basis of the available data regarding the capacity of its main items of germ-breeding equipment, that Detachment 731 alone was capable of breeding, in the course of one production cycle, lasting only a few days, no less than thirty quadrillion microbes. The experts stress that this is an extraordinarily large quantity of microbes to be produced in such a space of time.

One of the divisions of the eight was called the "Training and Education" Division. It trained its soldiers on skills related to the use of bacteriological weapons for combat units and sabotage groups.

Another division bred fleas, rats, mice, and other rodents to spread disease microbes, including plague, cholera, typhoid, and other germs for the mass genocide. According to a witness named Morita, Branch 543 in Hailar of Unit 731 had about 13,000 rats to spread microbe diseases.

According to Onoue's confession, his branch had caught and bred over 7,000 rats and bred fleas, as well as prepared 75 tons of materials to prepare the culture medium necessary to produce lethal bacteria: "I knew that Detachment 731 engaged in research and in the manufacture of large quantities of bacteriological weapons intended for use in bacteriological warfare against the Soviet Union. Branch 643, of which I was in charge, bred rodents and fleas which were sent to Detachment 731, where they were used for the manufacture of bacteriological weapons." This fact is also supported by an answer given during interrogation: "Major Onoue had applied to me on the desirability of having rats. I therefore wrote a letter saying that rats which were caught in the army units should not be killed, but sent to Major Onoue. I should explain that it was not convenient to say in the letter that the army units should go in for rat catching, and so it was put in the form of a suggestion that they should not kill the rats they caught, but send them to Branch 643."

## Chapter Five

# Human Experimentation as Described by the Defendants

Biological weapons were systematically tested by routine human experimentation conducted by the scientists working in the units. The humans used for experimentation were mostly Manchurians, Chinese, and Russians, according to the testimonies.

This is what Yamada Oota stated in his testimony regarding victims:

> "I... permitted them, and thereby virtually sanctioned the violent killing of Chinese, Russians, and Manchurians, who were sent for experimental purposes by the Kwantung Gendarmerie and by the Japanese Military Missions which were subordinated to me. ..."

Most of these prisoners were ordered to death by the Kempeitai, and they were sent to Unit 731 as test subjects to face their deaths as Furuichi testified, "... Detachment 731 experimented widely in the action of all lethal bacteria on human beings. For these purposes, we used imprisoned Chinese patriots and Russians whom the Japanese counterespionage service had condemned to extinction. ..."

In order to keep Unit 731 as a secret department and use the humans as test subjects, they needed to view the prisoners as not humans, but as logs or "maruta." This is what Witness Furuichi stated in his testimony: "... Detachment 731 had a special prison, where the persons designated for experimentation were kept under a strict regime and in close isolation; for purposes of secrecy, the detachment personnel usually referred to them as 'logs.'" During an interrogation on December 6th, 1949, defendant Kawashima Kiyoshi said, "To keep the prisoner experimentees, Detachment 731 had a special prison situated in the interior of the detachment's premises; here the experimentees were kept in strict isolation. The members of the detachment called the prisoners "logs." I myself frequently heard this term applied to the experimentees by the Chief of Detachment 731, General Ishii. Laboratory experiments on living people were performed by the 1st Division. In the spring of 1942, in addition to my other duties, I, for one month, acted as Chief of the 1st Division. The 1st Division conducted research work in the sphere of anti-epidemic measures, but the main object of this work was to devise the most effective means of bacteriological warfare; and it tested the final results of its work on living people who were confined in the prison which was part of the 1st Division."

In another interrogation on December 6th, 1949 of Kawasawa Tomio, he stated, "The bacteria that were produced under my direction were used for experiments to devise methods of disseminating bacteria under field conditions that were carried out on a proving ground especially equipped for this purpose at Anta Station. These experiments were performed on living people who were called 'logs.'"

There was a division assigned to test frostbite to better understand its cause and cure. During the trial, defendant Kajitsuka testified, "I first learned that researcher Yoshimura was working in Detachment 731 when I made my first visit of inspection to the detachment in March 1940. While examining the detachment's laboratories, I made the acquaintance of researcher Yoshimura. Here, in this laboratory, I learned that Yoshimura was engaged in investigating frostbite, in studying the causes leading to frostbite, in other words, the pathology of frostbite. I subsequently familiarized myself with Yoshimura's scientific work. Essentially, the idea was that the best way to cure frostbite was to immerse the frozen extremity in warm water at a temperature of 37°. From this I knew that Yoshimura was engaged in researches on frostbite."

As Kurakazu testified, "... On each floor, there were several rooms used as laboratories, and in the middle were the cells where the experimentees, or 'logs,' as Sergeant Major Tasaka told me they were called in the detachment, were kept... I remember clearly that, in addition to Chinese, there were Russians among the prisoners. In one cell I saw Chinese women... All the people kept in the cells had chains on their legs... Three Chinese had no fingers, and in the case of others, the finger bones could be seen... Yoshimura told me that this was the result of freezing experiments which he had been performing. ..."

According to witness Furuichi, "... A group of Russians, Manchurians, Chinese and Mongolians, with their legs in chains, were led out into the frost in parties of from two to sixteen and, on pain of being shot, were made to plunge their bare hands (one or both) into barrels of water, and then to keep their bare wet hands out in the frost for from ten minutes to two hours, depending on the temperature of the atmosphere. When freezing had set in, they were taken to the prison laboratory."

In another interrogation of defendant Kawashima Kiyoshi, he stated, "The 4th (production) Division, of which I was in charge from 1941 to 1943, was actually a factory for the manufacture of pathogenic germs. The Production Division was supplied with excellent apparatus for cultivating bacteria and this enabled us to produce monthly in a pure form about 300 kilograms of plague germs, or 500-600 kilograms of anthrax germs, or 800-900 kilograms of typhoid, paratyphoid or dysentery germs, or as much as 1,000 kilograms of cholera germs. Such quantities of bacteria were not actually produced every month, they were the calculated wartime requirements. Actually, the division produced bacteria in the quantities needed for the detachment's current work. For the purpose of testing the types of bacteriological weapons produced, and also of devising means of treating epidemic diseases, Detachment 731 constantly performed experiments on living people—Chinese and Russian prisoners, whom the Japanese Gendarmerie in Manchuria especially sent to the detachment for this purpose."

Witness Furuichi confirmed having infected human beings with typhoid, "... It was about the beginning of 1943 that, on the orders of Tabei, Chief of the 1st Division, I first took part in typhoid-infection experiments on people confined in the prison of Detachment 731. I prepared one liter of sweetened water, which I infected with typhoid germs. This liter I then mixed with more water, and this was administered to about 50 imprisoned Chinese, war prisoners, if I remember rightly, only some of whom had been inoculated against typhoid."

Unit 731 had an Anta testing ground where they also tested weapons used for biological warfare. The scientist in the trial who worked at Unit 731, Karasawa Tomio stated, "... I personally was present on two occasions at the Anta proving ground when the action of bacteria was tested on human beings under field conditions. The first time I was there towards the end of 1943, some ten persons were brought to the proving ground, were tied to stakes which had been previously driven into the ground five meters apart, and a fragmentation bomb was exploded by electric current about 50 meters away from them. A number of the experimentees were injured by bomb splinters and simultaneously, as I afterwards learned, infected with anthrax, since the bomb was charged with these bacteria... The second time I visited the proving ground was in the spring of 1944; about ten people were brought there, and, as on the first occasion, tied to stakes. A cylinder filled with plague germs was then exploded at a distance of roughly ten meters from the experimentees."

His colleague, Nishi Toshihide, also stated during the trial, "... In January 1945, in my presence, Lieutenant Colonel Ikari, Chief of the 2nd Division of Detachment 731, and Futaki, a research official of this division, performed an experiment at the detachment's proving ground near Anta Station in infecting ten Chinese war prisoners with gas gangrene. The ten Chinese prisoners were tied to stakes from 10 to 20 meters apart, and a bomb was then exploded by electricity. All ten were injured by shrapnel contaminated with gas gangrene germs, and within a week they all died in severe torment."

Through the various experiments of Unit 731, there was no way a prisoner could make it out alive, and they were killed on a mass scale. According to the accused Kawashima Kiyoshi, "... In the five years that the detachment was located at Pingfan Station, that is, from 1940 to 1945, not less than 3,000 persons passed through this death factory, and were killed by being infected with lethal bacteria. How many died before 1940, I do not know." This cruelty was confirmed by Mitomo Kazuo, who was a defendant in the trial and testified, "There was a case of a Russian on whom, in August 1944, various experiments were performed for two weeks. His constitution having broken down, Matsui ordered that he should be killed with an injection of potassium cyanide. ... On the pretext of giving him medical treatment, I made an injection ... of potassium cyanide, and the Russian died immediately. I made the injection in the solitary confinement cell. ... At the beginning of September 1944, two Russians were shot dead in my presence by a gendarme at the cattle cemetery, and were buried there. This was done on the orders of Lieutenant Nakajima. They were shot because no more experiments could be performed on them in view of their exhausted state and unsuitability for further experimentation."

He also experimented on Chinese citizens to see how they reacted: "At the end of August 1944, on the orders of Matsui, I put as much as a gram of heroin into some porridge and gave this porridge to an arrested Chinese citizen who ate it; about thirty minutes later he lost consciousness and remained in that state until he died 15-16 hours later. We knew that such a dose of heroin is fatal, but it did not make any difference to us whether he died or lived."

However, Chinese and Russians were not the only ones that were experimented on; Allied POWs were also tested to see how they would react to bacteriological weapons. According to a testimony by Karasawa on December 26th, "As far as I can recall, that was at the beginning of 1943. I was in hospital at the time in Mukden, and Minata, one of the researchers of the detachment, came to see me. He told me about his work, and said that he had come to Mukden to study immunity among

American war prisoners. Minata was sent specially by Detachment 731 to camps where Allied war prisoners were kept in order to study the immunity of Anglo-Saxons to infectious diseases."

Although Unit 100 was supposed to be doing experiments only related to animals, it was testing the bacteria on the prisoners. A laboratory assistant in Detachment 100, Hataki Akira, testified, "... Detachment 100 of the Kwantung Army was called an anti-epizootic unit, but actually it was a bacteriological unit, because it bred and cultivated the bacteria of glanders, anthrax and cattle plague, that is, the germs of epizootic diseases. Detachment 100 investigated the action of bacteria by means of experiments on domestic animals and human beings, for which purpose the detachment had horses, cows and other animals, and also kept human beings in its isolation cell, which I know from what I saw myself."

## Chapter Six

# Employment of the Bacteriological Weapon in the War

## China

During the trial, the Japanese imperialists admitted to their use of bacteriological weapons in the Pacific Asia War. Employing bacteriological weapons directly violated the Geneva Protocol of 1925 that was agreed to internationally. Primarily it was a "Protocol for the Prohibition of the Use in War of Asphyxiating, Poisonous or Other Gases, and of Bacteriological Methods of Warfare." The Japanese military branches, meanwhile, included facilities to produce bacteriological weapons in an efficient, fast-paced manner.

As Sato described during the interrogation of December 6th, 1949, "The output capacity of the Nanking Detachment Ei 1644 for the production of lethal bacteria was up to 10 kilograms per production cycle. To produce this quantity of bacteria, Detachment Ei 1644 had the following equipment: Ishii cultivators, about 200; incubator room, 1, dimensions 5X5X3 meters; 2 cylindrical autoclaves, 1.5 meters in diameter and 2.5 meters long;

incubators, about 40-50; steam sterilizers, 40-50, Koch boilers, about 40-50, and for cooking media, the detachment had large retorts, but how many I do not remember."

According to testimonies during the trial, a special bacteriological expedition commanded by General Ishii Shiro was dispatched to the theater of hostilities in Central China and Eastern China. According to the trial, the defendant Karasawa Tomio stated,

"... In the latter half of 1940, I was instructed by my immediate superior, Major Suzuki, to prepare 70 kilograms of typhoid bacteria and 50 kilograms of cholera bacteria. Major Suzuki told me that he had received instructions to prepare the bacteria from the Chief of the detachment, General Ishii, who was getting ready to organize a special expedition from the detachment to employ bacteria against the Chinese army... I carried out these orders. At the same time, I learned from personnel of the 2nd Division that that Division had bred five kilograms of plague-infected fleas as the carriers of this infection for the use of General Ishii's expedition. In September 1940, General Ishii, accompanied by a group of other officers of the detachment, left for Hankow, from which they returned in December 1940. The officers who had gone with General Ishii stated on their return to the detachment that the employment of plague-infected fleas had yielded good results. The dissemination of the fleas had caused a plague epidemic. One of the members of the expedition, Major Nozaki, showed me in proof of this a Chinese newspaper containing an article which reported that an outbreak of plague had occurred in the Nimpo area. The author of the article correctly concluded that the epidemic had been caused by the Japanese, since eyewitnesses had seen a Japanese plane flying over this area and dropping something from a low altitude. I read this article myself."

Another defendant, Kajitsuka, said, "Major General Kitano spoke of this in my office at the Headquarters of the Kwantung Army. No one else was present. He told me that a group of several men from Ishii's detachment had gone to an area south of Shanghai, taking with them the necessary materials, and had there disseminated plague fleas from the air, and that these experiments had proved effective. This was all he told me about the employment of the bacteriological weapon in China."

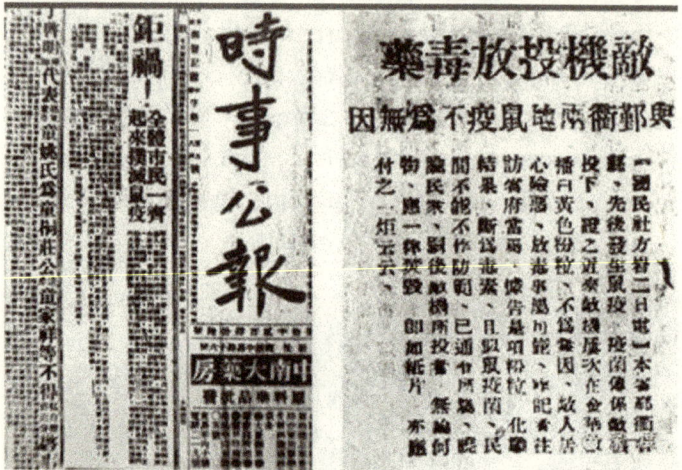

As the Imperial Japanese soldiers were retreating in Central China, Unit 731 launched an expedition. As Karasawa testified about preparing for the expedition, "... An expedition against the Chinese troops was carried out in the middle of 1942, with General Ishii in charge. ... As a preliminary to this expedition, 130 kilograms of paratyphoid and anthrax bacteria were prepared under my direction, again on the orders of Major Suzuki. According to my information, fleas were also used as epidemic carriers in this expedition. ... To carry out the expedition, General Ishii left with a party for Central China, where the Japanese troops were retreating at that time. The members of the expedition took advantage of the retreat to disseminate bacteria in the abandoned territory in order to cause outbreaks of epidemic among the advancing Chinese troops."

Another defendant, Kawashima Kiyoshi stated, "... In July 1942, after preliminary preparations had been made, the expedition left in several parties for Central China. ..."

"This time the bacteriological weapon was employed on the ground, the contaminating of the territory being done by sabotage action. ..."

"The advancing Chinese troops entered the contaminated zone and came under the action of the bacteriological weapon." Besides the confessions from the defendants, there was also evidence by a paper record of an order No. 659-HEI by General Umezu which instructed the Chief of the Field Railway to transport the Nara Detachment from the Kamo army unit. It was ordered that this unit with its 40 men and their baggages be transported to Central China.

極秘

關作命丙第六五九號

關東軍命令

關東軍野戰鐵道司令官ハ別紙

見表ニ據リ奈良部隊器材ノ鐵

輸送ヲ處理スヘシ

新京軍司令部
八月二十五日十七時

梅津中將

145

通報先

甲戊部隊、OTS、2GS、1GS、憲司

北支軍、支総軍 部内

The attacks on China were also verified by a report written by Frank S. Tavenner Jr., who was the chief counsel to the U.S. House Un-American Activities Committee. Check more on **pacificatrocities.org/tavenner-report**.

# USSR

KANTOKUEN, short for Kantogun Tokubetsu Enshu, which referred to Kwangtung Army Special Maneuvers, was an operational plan created by the Imperial Japanese Army. It was a plan to invade and occupy the far eastern region of the Soviet Union. The Imperial Japanese Army saw an opportunity after Nazi Germany's attack of the Soviet Union to conquer it as well. It was the most extensive Japanese military plan.

Part of the plan was to employ the heavy use of the chemical and biological weapons and to include seven Japanese armies to conquer the Soviet Union. According to the plan, the Imperial Japanese Army could defeat and destroy the Soviet Union within six months. However, Japan also needed to plan for its Southeast Asia attack, and the Japanese realized that Nazi Germany was not going to win Europe anytime soon, so decided to cancel the KANTOKUEN plan by September of 1941. However, they were set on their vision of employing biological weapons against the Soviet Union.

During an interrogation on December 6th, 1949, Zensaku confessed, "Being a veterinary surgeon, as a researcher, first in the 1st Section of the 2nd Division of the detachment, and later in the 6th Section of the same division formed in December 1943, I studied the action of glanders and anthrax germs, engaged in the breeding of these germs, and took part in devising all sorts of methods of using these germs in bacteriological warfare. For this purpose, in July-August 1942, I took part in an expedition, called 'summer maneuvers,' in the area of Tryokhrechye. The object of this expedition was to investigate the possibility of using anthrax and glanders germs under natural conditions approximating those in the area of anticipated hostilities—on the frontier of the Soviet Union. During this expedition, experiments were made in contaminating the river Derbul and water sources with glanders, and the soil and grass surface with anthrax. The germs for this purpose were cultivated in a field laboratory and tested on horses, sheep and guinea pigs.

From June 1944 onwards, I was with a group of researchers from Detachment 100 in North Khingan Province and, on the orders of the Command of the Kwantung Army, conducted reconnoitring operations for the
purpose of gaining information on the whereabouts and
number of cattle belonging to the inhabitants of the districts bordering on the Soviet Union and the Mongolian
People's Republic, on the condition of these cattle, the
whereabouts of summer and winter pastures and hayfields, and the condition of the roads and water sources.
The Japanese Command needed this information in
order, in the event of war against the Soviet Union, to
carry out the wholesale infection of cattle as a means of
bacteriological sabotage.

In this group, from June to September 1944, I carried
out a number of assignments on the orders of Captain
Asao, and from September 1944 to the day I was taken
prisoner (August 1945) I was in charge of this group for
Asao had been recalled. I knew from what I was told by
the Chief of Detachment 100, Major General Wakamatsu, that in conformity with the information I had col-
lected, aircraft were to spray the germs of glanders, anthrax and cattle plague for the purpose of infecting cattle
in the districts bordering on the Soviet Union and Mongolia in the event of war breaking out. Concerning the
work of my group I made two written reports to Major
General Wakamatsu, enclosing topographical maps giving reconnoitering results (condition of water sources,
pastures, cattle, etc.). On one occasion I made a verbal
report on the same subject to the Chief of the Veterinary

Service of the Kwantung Army, Lieutenant General Takahashi Takaatsu.

Furthermore, I gave information on the work performed to Chief of the Hailar Military Mission, Lieutenant Colonel Amano, who, as I had learned from Major General Wakamatsu, was aware of the assignments my group had received. I know that in his report to the Kwantung Army Headquarters, Lieutenant Colonel Amano commended the work we had done.

Simultaneously with the afore-mentioned work, I, on the orders of Major General Wakamatsu, in the summer of 1945 purchased from the inhabitants of North Khingan Province 500 sheep, 100 head of cattle and 90 horses with the 80,000 yen which had been assigned for this purpose. I knew from what Major General Wakamatsu had told me that in the event of war against the Soviet Union, the cattle were to be infected with anthrax and glanders and the sheep with sheep plague and, for sabotage purposes, left in the rear of the Soviet troops in order to cause outbreaks of severe infectious diseases. I knew that for this purpose the necessary quantities of the afore-mentioned germs were to be carried by aircraft to the places where the cattle I had bought would be, and the cattle were to be infected by sabotage groups formed for the purpose. I also plead guilty to the fact that while I was in North Khingan Province, I, on the orders of Major General Wakamatsu, purchased cattle (10 calves) to be used for experiments conducted early in the spring of 1945 in the region of the river South Khan-gol. I learned from Major Yamaguchi, who took part in these experiments, that during the experiments called 'winter maneuvers,' tests were made of the action of cattle-plague and sheep-plague germs under winter conditions by spraying these germs on the snow and on cattle feed scattered on the snow. These experiments were made under conditions similar to those under which bacteriological sabotage against the Mongolian People's Republic was to be conducted, for it is known that, in Mongolia, cattle gain their food in the winter time by grazing.

In addition to this, in the summer of 1943, with the object of ascertaining the amount of poison that was needed to kill horses (with potassium cyanide, strychnine, etc.), I, on the orders of Chief of the 2nd Division, Hasaka, experimented on 40-50 horses from units of the Kwantung Army. As a result of these experiments, ten horses died. I did not know for what purpose these experiments were made, but I presume that methods were being sought of using poisons for sabotage purposes."

According to the trial, Units 731 and 100 organized specialized training for officers and non-commissioned officers in the use of bacteriological weapons. Takahashi Takaatsu stated, "... After the 'Kan-Toku-En' operations plan appeared, 'epizootic' units were formed under the headquarters of every army in Manchuria. The chiefs of these units were medical men, expert bacteriologists, detailed from Detachment 100. ... The initiator of these units was the 1st Operations Division of the General Staff of the Japanese Army... The function of the epizootic units was to prepare for and conduct bacteriological warfare and sabotage against the Soviet Union. ...."

Defendant Kawashima testified as well on the intensification of preparation of bacteriological warfare in 1941, "... During one of my visits to General Ishii in the summer of 1941, after Germany had begun war on the Soviet Union, General Ishii, referring in the presence of divisional chiefs Lieutenant Colonel Murakami and Colonel Oota Akira to the need for intensifying the detachment's activities, read out to us an order of the Chief of the Japanese General Staff insisting upon the speeding up of research work on plague bacteria as a means of bacteriological warfare. The order made special mention of the need for the mass breeding of fleas as plague carriers."

Another defendant, Nishi, who worked at Unit 731 as the Chief of Training and Education, stated, "... By the time of Germany's attack on the Soviet Union in 1941 and the concentration of the Kwantung Army in Manchuria on the borders of the Soviet Union, the research work of Detachment 731 in the sphere of devising effective means of bacteriological attack had in the main been completed, and the detachment's activities were now directed to perfecting the process of mass production of bacteria and the means for their dissemination. It was established that plague bacteria were the most effective means of attack."

According to defendant Takahashi Takaatsu, who was working at Unit 100 during the war, "In the summer of 1942, on my orders, a group of men from Detachment 100, headed by researcher Ida Kiyoshi, experimented in the region of the river Derbul, in the Tryokhrechye area, in infecting animals to test the effectiveness of bacteriological weapons under climatic conditions most closely approximating those prevailing on Soviet Union territory."

Another defendant, Mitomo Kazuo, who voluntarily joined Unit 100 in April 1941 stated, "Furthermore, on many occasions I took part in experiments to test on animals and living people the effectiveness of the lethal bacteria I had cultivated in anticipation of their use by the Command of the Kwantung Army in war against the Soviet Union. Thus, in July-August 1942, I, with a group of researchers from Detachment 100, took part in an expedition in the area of Tryokhrechye, where the durability of glanders germs was tested in the river Derbul and of anthrax in stagnant water sources. This expedition was under the command of Chief of the 2nd Division of Detachment 100, Major Muramoto. There, too, I myself cultivated the germs of glanders and anthrax, which our group used for experiments on the river Derbul and in stagnant water sources. These tests were made ... on the river Derbul, which flows into the river Argun on the frontier of the U.S.S.R."

This account was confirmed by another defendant, Hirazakura Zensaku, during an interrogation: "In July-August 1942, I took part in an expedition, called 'summer maneuvers,' in the area of Tryokhrechye. The object of this expedition was to investigate the possibility of using anthrax and glanders germs under natural conditions approximating to those in the area of anticipated hostilities—on the frontier of the Soviet Union. During this expedition, experiments were made in contaminating the river Derbul and water sources with glanders, and the soil and grass surface with anthrax. The germs for this purpose were cultivated in a field laboratory and tested on horses, sheep and guinea pigs.

From June 1944 onwards, I was with a group of researchers from Detachment 100 in North Khingan Province and, on the orders of the Command of the Kwantung Army, conducted reconnoitering operations for the purpose of gaining information on the whereabouts and number of cattle belonging to the inhabitants of the districts bordering on the Soviet Union and the Mongolian People's Republic, on the condition of these cattle, the whereabouts of summer and winter pastures and hayfields, and the condition of the roads and water sources. The Japanese Command needed this information in order, in the event of war against the Soviet Union, to carry out the wholesale infection of cattle as a means of bacteriological sabotage."

## Chapter Seven

# Destroying Evidence of Unit 731

On August 8th, 1945, two days after the dropping of the atomic bomb, but a week before the official surrender of Japan issued by Emperor Hirohito, the Soviet Union fought a decisive battle with the Japanese in Northern Manchuria to free the colony from the Japanese Empire. Most civilian and military compounds were destroyed by fire, and the Japanese soldiers retreated to Hailin, Linkow, Sunyu, and Hailar. During their hasty retreat, the Japanese did a mediocre job of hiding dead bodies. On the outskirts of Hailar, the Soviets found at least 10,000 dead bodies, and it was the same in Harbin, with live rabbits, guinea pigs, livestock, and other cattle in cages.[1]

However, not only was most evidence destroyed hastily, personnel were also handed potassium cyanide as Japan was nearing loss of the war. According to the interrogation of defendant Nishi Toshihide who destroyed Branch 673 of Unit 731 in Sunyu, "On August 11-12, 1945, owing to the advance of the Soviet Army, and with the object of concealing the fact that weapons for conducting bacteriological warfare had been manufactured

---

[1] Factories of Death p. 3-4.

in the Japanese Kwantung Army and that Branch 673 of Detachment 731 under my command had been involved in these criminal activities, on my orders all the branch's service premises and living quarters, equipment, materials and documents were destroyed by fire, and for the same purpose, on my orders, on August 14, 1945, poison in the shape of potassium cyanide was issued to the entire personnel (120 men) to be taken by them to commit suicide in the event of the danger arising of their being captured by the Soviet forces."

Another defendant, Onoue Masao, who was the Chief of Branch 643 of Unit 731 in Hailin confirmed, "By order of Lieutenant General of the Medical Service Ishii, Chief of Detachment 731, on August 13, 1945, I destroyed by fire Branch 643 with all its materials, equipment and documents, except for the code and 20-25 grams of fleas, which I sent to the headquarters of Detachment 731. What the command of Detachment 731 had in view in ordering the branch to be destroyed by fire, I do not know. I knew that Detachment 731 engaged in devising and manufacturing large quantities of means of bacteriological warfare, such as the germs of plague, anthrax and other lethal bacteria, which were tested on living people, for which purpose the detachment had an inner prison and a proving ground where the experiments were performed. In the spring of 1944, I, together with the Chief of the General Division of Detachment 731, travelled by aeroplane to the proving ground where experiments were to have been made in practically testing bacteriological weapons on living people; but owing

to the fact that the command of the detachment can-
celled the experiments, for reasons unknown to me, I
flew back to the detachment's headquarters next day."

## Chapter Eight

# Punishment

Due to the lack of physical evidence, it was difficult for the prosecutors to depend solely on confessions and hearsay testimony. However, the trial verdict declared that defendants were all guilty and sentenced them to labor camp from 2-25 years. There was a suspicion that the scientists traded in their scientific research in exchange for more lenient punishments.

The sentences of the following were announced by Major General of Jurisprudence D. CHERTKOV, Colonel of Jurisprudence M. ILNITSKY, and Lieutenant Colonel of Jurisprudence VOROB YOV:

**Yamada Otozoo**, on the basis of Art. 1 of the Decree of the Presidium of the Supreme Soviet of the U.S.S.R. of April 19, 1943, to confinement in a labor correction camp for a term of twenty-five years.

**Kajitsuka Ryuji**, on the basis of Art. 1 of the Decree of the Presidium of the Supreme Soviet of the U.S.S.R. of April 19, 1943, to confinement in a labor correction camp for a term of twenty-five years.

**Takahashi Takaatsu**, on the basis of Art. 1 of the Decree of the Presidium of the Supreme Soviet of the U.S.S.R. of April 19, 1943, to confinement in a labor correction camp for a term of twenty-five years.

**Kawashima Kiyoshi**, on the basis of Art. 1 of the Decree of the Presidium of the Supreme Soviet of the U.S.S.R. of April 19, 1943, to confinement in a labor correction camp for a term of twenty-five years.

**Nishi Toshihide**, on the basis of Art. 1 of the Decree of the Presidium of the Supreme Soviet of the U.S.S.R. of April 19, 1943, to confinement in a labor correction camp for a term of eighteen years.

**Karasawa Tomio**, on the basis of Art. 1 of the Decree of the Presidium of the Supreme Soviet of the U.S.S.R. of April 19, 1943, to confinement in a labor correction camp for a term of twenty years.

**Onoue Masao**, on the basis of Art. 1 of the Decree of the Presidium of the Supreme Soviet of the U.S.S.R. of April 19, 1943, to confinement in a labor correction camp for a term of twelve years.

**Sato Shunji**, on the basis of Art. 1 of the Decree of the Presidium of the Supreme Soviet of the U.S.S.R. of April 19, 1943, to confinement in a labor correction camp for a term of twenty years.

**Hirazakura Zensaku**, on the basis of Art. 1 of the Decree of the Presidium of the Supreme Soviet of the

U.S.S.R. of April 19, 1943, to confinement in a labor correction camp for a term of ten years.

**Mitomo Kazuo**, on the basis of Art. 1 of the Decree of the Presidium of the Supreme Soviet of the U.S.S.R. of April 19, 1943, to confinement in a labor correction camp for a term of fifteen years.

**Kikuchi Norimitsu**, on the basis of Art. 1 of the Decree of the Presidium of the Supreme Soviet of the U.S.S.R. of April 19, 1943, to confinement in a labor correction camp for a term of two years.

**Kurushima Yuji**, on the basis of Art. 1 of the Decree of the Presidium of the Supreme Soviet of the U.S.S.R. of April 19, 1943, to confinement in a labor correction camp for a term of three years.

Furthermore, all of the prisoners were repatriated to Japan by 1956 except for Tomio Karasawa, who committed suicide right before his scheduled return to Japan. Most of the scientists who worked at Unit 731 were able to obtain high ranking positions in corporations or government, since they had likely traded their research work for immunity from life imprisonment.

For an extended version of this trial, visit

**http://www.pacificatrocities.org/khabarovsk-selected.html**

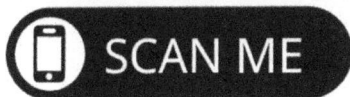

SCAN ME

www.ingramcontent.com/pod-product-compliance
Lightning Source LLC
Chambersburg PA
CBHW032054040426
42449CB00007B/1105